Pain Demands To Be Felt

Keenal Majithia

BookLeaf Publishing

India | USA | UK

Presentation by *BookLeaf Publishing*

Web: www.bookleafpub.com

E-mail: info@bookleafpub.com

ISBN: 9789357446365

First edition 2022

DEDICATION

To people who feel more like Neville Longbottom, instead of Harry Potter. You are brave, you can fight for what you believe in, just like he did.

ACKNOWLEDGEMENT

To everyone who's taken the time (before this book!) to read my poems, and to have a little faith that I know what I'm doing with a pen (or keyboard!)

Obscurity

Obscurity.

The state of being unknown, inconspicuous, or unimportant.

Unimportant, insignificant…small.

It's an unconscious fear

Something we wish to never hear.

Something people will never tell us.

'You'll be president someday, cure cancer, bring peace to the Middle East'

….No. Chances are you won't matter much before you're deceased.

Who knows when you'll reach the final sentence in your story?

Not everyone achieves worldly glory.

Yes, you may be able to fantasise

But

It's impossible to…

Organise.

People attempt to plan their lives

But things pop up when they least expect.

This meticulousness brings them great comfort

It's like a cloak of invincibility.

As if death will think they're special enough to
leave alone.

Who are they kidding?

So if we're so minuscule in the grand scheme of
things,

Why are we here in the first place?

And don't say God, because this omniscient
omnipotent being is reserved for post death.

Tornado

I feel lost
Slightly b r ok e n inside
As if something's been smashed to smithereens
Or the rock pumping my blood is slowly
imploding

Yet there's a burning sensation
A fickle yet encouraging ray of hope
Deceptive? Probably.
But not enough to stop me waiting for
something ExtraOrdinary
Which will help break the barriers
I built around me

Hush the tears
Dry the screams
Stop the confusion!
Surrounding my crazy delusions

What am I waiting for to take me away?
Away from the disappointment, abuse,
subordination, anxiety…
But this begs the question,
Why don't I just leave?
Or do we have no fREe wILl in this society

And is even 'nothing' determined by everything
else?

My hands are handcuffed
As three parallel rivers stream down my face
The invisible padlock against my lips feeling
rigid and cold
And like a tornado
I lack any ounce of control I may have had
But that's only because I lack

direction
Because I have no idea what or
where or who I should be

Expectations.
What will you achieve by reading this poem?
Not much, probably.
What do I achieve by existing?
Not much, probably.
Would I achieve anything by stopping though?
Not, much…probably?

I just want to find my destination
But I'm filled with anger and hesitation
So I can't really enjoy the journey
Unless I use medication or attempt meditation

But what do I know?

It's late and I'm irate
Feel like I've been locked up in a box
Squashed, moulded and cast by someone else
Then chucked into outer space
My mind has been sucked out but I'm left with a
twisted soul.
Damaged goods, I am.

I don't expect you to understand
But I'm sure some of you can relate,
If you've ever been a 17 year old
Feeling slightly out of

place.

Bullying Amplified

It's like…being afraid to speak out
Like having a zip on your mouth
That the tormentor constantly plays with
And it's like always having doubts
As you wonder, is it your fault?

You think one day it will stop.
The torrent of words which hit you like an axe,
The constant teasing behind your back.
You even consider
Wanting to disappear.

But one day that bully moves away
You begin to cheer, hip hip hooray!
But then you go to school the next day
And there's a replacement by Tuesday.

Except this time there's more scars involved.
The manipulation is more intricate,
The bar has been raised.
It's the person you never expected
So you're a little fazed.

All you can do is hide in your school jumper,
Wishing it would act as a barrier.

You have marks on your arms, tinged with blue
It's all over your arms like a disease
Screaming to be seen
For someone to recognise.

You realise the bruises are braver than you,
Because they scream and shout
While you keep quiet
And silently pray for things to change.

Then when you go to secondary school it does.
The number of students multiply
And so does the teasing.
Although it's more diluted now,
It's far more fleeting

Slowly, you build up a spine
And tell people to fuck of.
You're no longer a poor little mime.
You're finally happy
For a decent amount of time.

But the world wouldn't be satisfied without a
full circle
So it's time for sixth form
And many moments of misery inducing
mockery.
An assembly full of students sniggering behind
your back.

Calling you an un-talented hack.
Wishing you could hide again
Preferably in a large sack.

The one thing I needed in all of these situations
Was confrontation.
Rise above it,
Like a butterfly
And buzz by, leaving them to feel the sting

Which I did in the end.
Let's just hope it doesn't happen again.

What Are We Allowed To Be?

'You can be anything you want to be!' they said.
'You'll grow up to be smart, successful and happy.'
Yeah, that's what I'm talking about, I thought.
'You'll go to university, get a proper job, and make lots of money…'
Ok, calm down now. What if I wanna be rapper like Dappy?
'then you'll get married to the perfect man, have 2.5 kids, a big house, settle down and be close enough for us to pop around.'
What if I meet a woman instead? Or a man that's nothing like Superman?
Or I don't want kids because that's not for me?
Or I choose to foster or adopt.
After all, It's my decision for what I opt.
And as for settling down, what if I want to travel and live in a caravan?
Or if I work as a barman,
Or my dream is to be like Wu tang clan.
Or if I want to live in Japan,
Or fight as a soldier in Afghanistan.

'We'll make sure you're successful and happy,
And help you decide what you want to do by the
time you're 16!'
So now there's a deadline?
And if I miss it, apparently the future will be my
fine!
I know you want a smile on my face
So you'll raise me lovingly and try your best.
But remember life is not a race.
And what if your definition of successful is not
the path I wish to take?
What is it somebody once said about the road
less travelled?
I want that road, or to create a new one, maybe
several.
I want life to constantly fill my head with more
memories, adventures and knowledge,
Because it's not just about the destination.
And maybe I'll be no good at tests,
But be a brilliant jest.
Maybe I'll be a policewoman in a bright vest.
Maybe I'll drop out of uni and create a blood
test
That diagnoses 30 types of illnesses in the west,
Or Dragon's Den chooses me as the one in
which they invest.
Whatever I do or become,
I highly doubt there is just one path,
I may love to do sums,

But if I don't go to uni, don't label me as dumb.
If I want to be a plumber then teach me about
apprenticeships
It's one of the highest paying jobs after all,
So I'll end up far from just serving chips
And tell my teachers if I'm saying words aloud,
I'm not trying to disrupt the class,
I just learn differently, acoustically
That's something we need to recognise,
So our national curriculum can be more
individualised
Yes I realise its hard work, maybe a bit costly,
But if we're the future, aren't we worth it?
And if we're the first generation that's less well
off than our parents with opportunities,
Then clearly something has to change.
Someone needs to think sensibly and
pragmatically but also slightly emotionally.
Not just increase our tuition fees and tell us there
are 'other opportunities'
That will just increase animosity.
What about actually showing us how to get to
these other paths?
Tell me that being a runner will increase my
chances of being an actor
Or that I can get promoted to a higher position
with experience, not just a degree.
Or teach and assess me in a way that doesn't just
test my memory during exam time.

And get people that know students to present
ideas in parliament instead of relying on twisted
statistics and Michael Gove.
Put teachers in charge of the curriculum that is
implemented in our kid's education
And don't just make it all about achieving first
place in the league tables,
Until your integrity is disabled.
Instead of a lesson being solely devoted to bleak
exam technique,
Because this is highly concerning.

So, if I can truly be whatever I want to be,
Please, teach us, support us and listen to us.
Because our lost generation will need it,
With around 30% unemployed, not in education
or following their own dreams.
Think of their self-esteem.
The only generation to be growing up faster due
to this media exposure
But at the same time growing up slower,
With more people than ever depending on their
parents till their 30.
So help us to appreciate life and also be our
versions of successful,
Because this is essential so that we are no longer
resentful
And so we'll be lost no more and find ourselves.

Fight or Flight

Hands shaking, palms sweating
Heart beating, mouth drying
The acute stress response system starts kicking
in
Slowly, the words I'm meant to say, I start
forgetting
This has happened so often, I find it tiring

There's no microphone, no stage, no camera to
record me
At least that bits comforting
The scars from last time are all too vivid
So for a long time, I cried and hid

The views online gave them ammunition
The shares on Facebook felt like being shot with
a rifle
At school, they tore me down guerrilla warfare
style
Except not with guns and grenades
But with humiliation, teasing and whispering

It sucks to know I could have prevented the
ignition

By not uploading something online the whole
world could see
Never did I know people could be so childish
and vile
Or that pointing and laughing could feel like a
thousand blades
Oh, and don't forget those provoking fake
smiles.

Of course, I've learnt something from then
One excruciatingly bad experience won't form a
pattern
Unless you let it happen
And even then it's probably due to a
self-fulfilling prophecy
Not something you can see empirically
So once you fall, get up graciously
And if you fall again, invest in a helmet and
keep getting back up

So where was i?
Autonomic nervous system kicking in
Adrenaline gushing through my veins
But this time I'm not going to flee
I'm going to FIGHT.

#MeToo

Me too.
I think. How much do I have to have been
subjected to, to be part of the subject?
How many times do I have to be objectified and
ogled at till I am purely seen as an object?

How far do the unwanted touches have to go for
the merely queasy feeling I get in the pit of my
stomach to be valid enough before I call
attention to this incident?
Why can't you tell him to respect me, instead of
expect me to be constantly vigilante?
Do you honestly think I'm making this up and
simply being insolent?
You don't see that he is forcing himself upon me
in an attempt to prove he is not impotent?
You don't see that he's exerting power any way
he can so as to not feel insignificant?
Even if that means my mind's imprisonment.

Long after my body has been released from
captivity.
And don't fucking tell me this is simply a
natural proclivity that's basically evolutionary.

When 83 year old women like Sonja Fischer are being repugnantly raped, as the perpetrators strip them simultaneously of their cashmere cardigans and dignity, whilst they barely have clarity.

And that is in California. It doesn't only happen to India's daughters, but all of Gaia's daughters. Why do we call these lines blurred when all you need to do is open your eyes and the haziness will sharpen like a knife?

Make Up

Eyelash curler. Make me look sharp.

Eyeliner. Define my eyes.

I want people to be surprised, change their perspective.

A touch of blush. Make my cheeks more definitive.

Cover up my pasty skin so people see I have emotions.

Though it appears embarrassment or humiliation may be more pronounced,

As the pink tinge should suggest if naturally occurring,

But this artificial hue exudes a manufactured air of confidence, of well-put-togetherness.

Concealer, of course, to hide and suppress your secrets,

Close the door on those skeletons

Whether they're only the size of hills or
mountains,

It's something you want to retain.

It's not just because you're vain.

And lipstick. A pink or maroon if you just want
to blend in.

Just to accentuate your grin.

Perhaps a red if you're planning to head to bed
or get ahead.

It's the bolder decision as if not pulled of
correctly,

May receive derision or an opinion division.

So there you have it, a 21st century mask.

Some call it an art to applaud, others are
appalled,

And few are jealous if they can't afford

The best or have to reveal a tiny portion of
themselves.

They feel pressured to conceal and not be real,

Not show how they really feel and hide behind
this façade

Just to prove they're hard.

Beauty

Look at me.
What do you see?
A tall slender white woman?
That means I've won the genetic lottery,
According to the majority of society that view
me.
History has left a legacy that may not be as
visible,
But like phantom limbs, still remain.

What if you looked at me and saw a beige girl
trying to become a model?
Make me your token Tyra
So you can fill your 4% 'coloured' quota?
Or indirectly discriminate and tell me I don't
have 'the look'?
Of course the 2010 Equality act makes it evident
we've come a long way,
But there are still biased people we encounter
every day.

They think they're right,
Think in terms of black and white,
And don't acknowledge the varying shades of
grey,

Are beautiful too.
What if I was shaped like an apple or
minute-glass?
Ironically if I was big boned, I'd get told to shed
my fat,
But if I was obese this would be politically
incorrect.
How is that?

How can society have this double standard
where some women are criticized,
For not being the right size,
Yet we have a small number who find it ok,
To have thighs unhealthily made out of fries?
You don't know where on the scale from 0 to
100 you belong,
Because whatever you are, you'll think at some
point its wrong.
And after seeing Beyoncé claim black is
beautiful,
You'll wonder why you hear of her wearing
lightening cream.
You'll see Kate moss traipsing along the street
And realize in photos she's been airbrushed from
her head to feet.

Don't be surprised when you realize this affects
78% of girls self-esteem,

Influencing them to reach some unattainable
ideal of perfection,
Making it their lifelong dream.
And industries play on their insecurities,
As corporations try to sell various amenities,
Advertising products that change your
recognisability,
Without realising the grave severity.

Instead why can't society advocate that it's who
you are that makes you great.
Beauty is not in your shade of melanin or size,
It is something which radiates from inside,
Thus giving you that warm glow on the outside,
Using your heart and soul as a basis,
For a more valid judgement of beauty.

Murder

She quietly slips away
For a few minutes everyday
Tells herself she's having a good day

She climbs the steps discreetly
The first time she tried it, oh how her heart was
beating
It was like the sound of a drum
Thump thump thump
It made her look around and run

Later on she received purple scars
Making her miss the sound of the drum
She sees the purple so much
When it happens, her heart barely makes a hum
The pain sits on the surface
No longer entrenching this now hollow drum
For she has now become numb

The drum which once produced joyful noise
And made people dance
Has now been replaced with a poisonous voice
And she occasionally appears to be in a trance.

Not letting people see

She goes through daily motions like an Oscar
winner
But when she gets home,
He beats her with a stick because she's the
breadwinner?
Yet demands she cook his dinner
Berates her into being thinner
Manipulates her into thinking she's the sinner

All alone in the house, no one
to stick up for her

And at work, she does everything she can so the
monotonous hummmm
Of the drum is hidden
Covered by the joyful tunes they all appear to
know
With concealer the scars can be hidden
When asked to go out past sunset,
She cannot say it is forbidden
So fakes an ailment, pretending to be bedridden

But soon the drum top begins to crack
People see behind the Duchenne smile
It becomes too much to hack
Her friend's number she begins to dial
She's busy, says she'll call back in a while
The overwhelming feeling of numb
This humdrum…

Abused into staying mum
By the one she must dutifully call mum
Not being able to say a word to the one she
lovingly calls mum

Causes

Her

To

Jump

A decision

Which she

Can no

Longer

Take back

Because He took away

SHE.

Natural Love

A person may experience many things in life
Yet in many cases
The greatest life experiences just happen to a
person
Without any action required on behalf of them

It is passive
Uncontrolled by anything of empirical existence
Simply willed by something pure, natural
Or even spiritual, if you will

Some may say this force is so hidden
It only lives inside a safe buried in the depths of
the ocean
Or that it is so undetectable
That it must be absolutely fictional

Logic is their best friend
And they see anything else as a dead end
True, it is possible they are right
But they don't even consider the possibility they
are wrong

Like the large majority who thought the earth
was flat

Or the many individuals who thought the Titanic
was unsinkable
They refuse to be proven wrong
Due to…shame?

Or is it because they don't find what they are
looking for
At the time that suits them
Or in the right place
Sometimes even with the wrong person

That's the thing about nature
It accepts the fact that it can be as wrong as
A sky diver without a parachute
But it's prepared to take that leap

And when it's right
It can be as beautiful and tender
As a birdsong at 6am in a pink clouded June
morning
But it happens on its own terms

Attempting to ensure near perfection can be a
lengthy process
So stick your nose out of it and let love happen
to you
Forget about matchmakers, shaadi dot com or
interfering aunties
Just leave it to the master.

A Life in Trainers

Look at where your footsteps have gone,
The prints they've left behind,
The excitement they've felt,
The blood and sweat they've had trickling out of
them into a pair of sole's.

Expose your shoes to the elements.
Let them breathe, soak up life,
Fire up a dance floor, walk the earth.

Wear them out
Till your feet scream and shout.
Explore.
Make your own trail,
Even if at first you fail.
Get off the beaten track,
Discover the mansions as well as the shacks.

Make sure they have a good grip so they're
planted firmly on the ground,
This way it will be easier to get around,
And if you get lost, you'll be easily found.

Wear them out,
Till your shoes scream and shout,
Till there's no soul left to make a sound.

The Motherland

For the first time in 17 years out of 18
I step into the motherland, and I see. Clearly.

No longer are my ears the sole point for the
knowledge I have
Of the corruption, the culture, the colourful
landscapes
It's truly an assault on the senses,
And there is know escape.

As soon as you land, the rickshaw drivers
attempt to scam you
A scooter simultaneously zips past, whilst my
eyes remain in awe
Cars horning as people, cows, goats even dodge
And I swear to you, its like nothing I ever saw

Hands reaching out to you begging for a rupee
Grateful if you even give five
And they go back to their make shift hut near the
old tree
Right next to a maharani's mansion
Because if you're wealthy you can live so care
free

Here, maids and housekeepers wait on you hand
and foot
The cook up delicious feasts of tasty food
And those outside, just nearby, are covered in
soot
You wonder where they get their fortitude.

On the way to the local market, I see a child.
She looks impoverished and asks for change,
But I'm told not to give too much, in case it's a
ruse,
I give a little and she smiles, my heart weeps
after our exchange.

Shortly after, I see the same child in an
orphanage,
And I wish I could give her the world.
I'm thankful she has a roof, even though in this
day and age,
There needs to be a transformation, a
metamorphosis.

Because in the same country,
I got to stay in a stately, former palace.
This is a curious country, where many are warm
hearted, generous,
But others just seem cold, and a little bit callous.

I've barely scratched the surface of my
motherland,
I've still yet to explore a great deal more,
There's still things about the country I
misunderstand,
So perhaps this poem is even a little premature.

A World Transformed

Eerily empty streets punctuated with people in
small pockets.
Grocery stores, off licenses and takeaways are
the only establishments that draw a breath.
They're the only places reaping any kind of the
profits,
Amidst a row full of shutters, to help slow the
rate of burgeoning death.

It's Saturday night and with few people scattered
around,
I take in familiar sights with a renewed
perspective.
Like a tourist mistakenly stumbling upon an
unnervingly bleak town,
That's been transformed by the recent
government directive.

Iridescent shades of marigold and marmalade
pour out of windows,
With life carrying on fervently – now more than
ever – on the inside.

Only peering outside at 8pm on Thursdays to
clap for our heroes.
Other than that, Houseparty, Zoom, and the
garden is where they temporarily reside.

Deliveroo drivers have stepped in (2 metres
apart) to feed the nation.
They gather in distanced formations around
chicken and kebab eateries, waiting patiently,
Whilst the once reliable Chinese takeaway
across the road is empty and faces degradation.
It's forced into the shadows shamefully, as
luminous lights of nearby eateries blaze
brazenly.

Strolling down the pavement, I see someone
approaching from the opposite direction.
My pulse intensifies as we briefly lock eyes,
teetering on opposite edges of the pathway,
As we nod in acknowledgement of what we're
doing for our protection at the intersection,
Eternally grateful there was no hint of a cough
and we both passed rapidly without delay.

I scan a supermarket that's still open and find
myself noticing their lack of floor tape.
I wince as two employees' shoulders nearly
touch as they chatter without a mask or barrier,

And notice a lack of social distancing in some
narrow aisles, my expression agape,
Apprehensively making mental notes on rules
that should be implemented in the shop interior.

I feel my phone vibrate thinking 'must be fake
news in the family WhatsApp again'
Take a moment to appreciate I can be outside for
this daily exercise,
Deeply inhale a breath as I let it go, meditatively
repeating to prevent going insane.
As a thought occurs; how clean was that air back
there? Will that cause my demise?

As my walk is coming to an end, I slow down
before returning to the comfortable prison,
And berate myself as I'm lucky to not be
working in a supermarket or hospital AKA 2020
battlefields.
I wonder if like a phoenix we'll arise from the
ashes of this, with a new found wisdom,
And how long the word will be like this, before
it is healed.

The birds singing, pollution levels dwindling,
cleaner waters are temporary,
Unless after covid, we take a new emboldened
approach to climate change.

The new found community spirit shown by
volunteers has pulled us together as we face this
common adversity,

And now that we know our neighbours, we
should go back to a post-covid world estranged.
Those currently working remotely have been
given a blessing in disguise now knowing being
in the office is not necessary.

A better work life balance could most easily be
arranged.
Even spending more quality time with your
family in your sanctuary may currently feel
revolutionary,
As we secretly are finding ways we like and
appreciate that small change.

Of course the horrors of this illness that plague
us are abysmal and scary.
The economic, health and mortality fears have
run many of us ragged with uncertainty,
But if we can take some lessons with us, we
could try to do something extraordinary.
Put the earth and our humanity equally at the
forefront and respect each other's liberties,
And transform our communities, climate, and
careers post covid-19 with dignity.

Searching

Searching for an answer
Isn't always easy
The more I tend to look
The deeper I fall
Into uncharted territory

The pixelated computer screens
And thick leather-bound hardbacks
Feel of little use

The thing that I'm searching for
Cannot be tested, experimented
Verified or even denied

The corners of my mouth begin to fall
Dark bags under my eyes start to form
The pace of my feet slows down
Till I can barely bother to drag them up anymore

Everyone thinks they know,
And fight to the death whether they're wrong or
right,
Extremists use it to defend your embryos
Over the people's rights of whom they belong
too.

But it also allows the kind-hearted to assemble,
It's their driver to do good, be better, find
salvation,
And at the faint hint of a sign, they tremble,
With joy, celebration, and elation!

I'm not quite sure exactly where I sit.
I think there is something.
Not all knowing or all powerful, I admit.
But it's something.

Something that galvanizes the birds to sing,
Forces the first flowers to bloom in spring,
Breathes beauty into the oceans where people go
snorkelling
And provides this glorious Earth to reside in.

So, I think I'll stop searching for the answer,
This incomprehensible spirit isn't in charge of
me anyway,
Besides, with this particular question, who's
ever made headway?
I'll find out when it's my time, someday.

Thirsty

Thirsty…
Desperately seeking, dreaming of a refreshing
glass of water.
I take the interminable trek
Far enough to feel like I'm in Quebec
But it's worth it because I know longer feel like
a wreck

I consume an extended sip
And feel ecstatic as soon as it touches my lips,
And feel it drip, drip down from the tip

Of my tongue into my system
until I feel like I'm back on top of the kingdom.
After the sip, I have a momentary think,
Reflect on how I neglect
What I have and regret

How this world is so
divided.
Some people have a bucketful and are so
excited!
And there are those whom have as life of
unease,
They walk for miles till their arms and feet are
tired

Only to be greeted with cholera infested, disease

Mixed with several drops of H20
It makes zero sense
This is rich land, where things are meant to grow
Colonialism ruined this place in the name of
shillings and cents
Everything that should be here, they pretty much
stole.

Leaving behind a legacy of…well, nonsense,
No one's ever received reparations,
Some of our governments pretend history was
different in a damaging game of pretence
Their money is shovelled into unnecessary
military defence

Or sending billionaires on holiday to the moon,
Meaning those worst off don't get water until
there's a monsoon.
I'm not preaching as if I could solve this
disparity in an afternoon,
I'm just still thirsty, insufferably so, this noon,
Desperately seeking, dreaming of a refreshing
glass of…
Change.
The tide is turning,
but my heart is burning,
Yearning,

For that day, we can all be as refreshed, as privileged, as I.

Living

Standing at the window pane
Gazing intently at the cerulean sky
Watching and waiting
For the days to go bye

For that day to come
When the world says welcome
And I can discover this earth

Jumping out of a jet
Climbing Kilimanjaro
Peering in the pyramids

It's not just a dream
It's my upcoming reality
That I will ensure
And take my slightly obscure
Yet life changing world tour

I don't want to be stuck
In a mundane rut
Which includes the notorious 9-5

I want to leap into the unknown
I don't want to be a robot

Or a clone

My eyes don't see what you see
I see beauty in mystery
You see certificates and success

You might call it optimism
Or naivety
But I'm calling it bravery
Because that's what it takes
To be different in this society

Leaping, running, gliding, flying
Is what I want to do
Tear up the map
Pick up my feet
And go.

I don't want to survive
I want to live.

Beside Me

I open my eyes and you're not here
I close my eyes and you're next to me
The crowd should cheer for me, not jeer
Because I feel your presence here with me
Not lazing about on the settee

I open my mouth to sing my song
And remember your supporting smile
What could possibly go wrong?
Besides the judge looking absolutely vile
Because I have tremendous style

As the first words come out
I start sweating like a pig
I hope no one starts to shout
Or claim this contest is rigged
Or my tongue might fall of like a twig

My eyes are super glued to the door
Hoping you will somehow show
Even though you'd probably find it a bore
You'd be here to say go girl, go!

And then as if a miracle
From the corner of my eye, I see your face

And my song finally sounds lyrical
I knew you'd turn up without being chased
With you here I can win this race.

Perfect Harmony

Your care for each other is seen as soon as you
both wake
As you have your first phone call of the day
Your partnership is a true meeting of the minds
Like yin and yang, you both synchronize
Your joy is seen when you sing along with each
other in the car
Or when you're both dancing together at the bar

Both in perfect harmony
Simultaneously best friends and life partners so
effortlessly
It's not just from all of this, that I know you'll
love each other till you're old and grey
But from how you look at each other, still in the
same way
As you did 7 years ago, so effervescently

Your love is not just as beautiful as a flower in
full bloom
But it's as strong as the roots they grow from
You both make a perfect bride and groom
And from today, you'll embark on the most
marvelous adventure,
In which your compassion will never falter.

Thus it is inconceivable that you could ever part
Because since you first met, your roots have
gradually entwined
The threads of your hearts have gradually been
sewn together
And the two of you have become seamlessly
aligned.
I wish you both years of marital bliss.
Rich with laughter, tenderness and happiness.